BLAZERS

U.S. MILITARY WEAPONS AND ARTILLERY

by Carol Shank

CONTENT CONSULTANT:
MAJOR (RET.) MARGARET GRIFFIN, MS
U.S. ARMY
ATLANTA, GEORGIA

READING CONSULTANT:
BARBARA J. FOX
READING SPECIALIST
PROFESSOR EMERITA
NORTH CAROLINA STATE UNIVERSITY

CAPSTONE PRESS
a capstone imprint

Blazers is published by Capstone Press,
1710 Roe Crest Drive, North Mankato, Minnesota 56003.
www.capstonepub.com

Library of Congress Cataloging-in-Publication Data
Shank, Carol.
    U.S. military weapons and artillery / by Carol Shank; content consultant, Margaret Griffin;
reading consultant, Barbara J. Fox.
    p. cm. — (Blazers. U.S. military technology)
    Includes index.
    Audience: Grades 4-6.
    ISBN 978-1-4296-8614-3 (library binding)
    ISBN 978-1-62065-214-5 (ebook PDF)
1. United States. Army—Artillery—Juvenile literature. 2. Artillery—Juvenile literature.
3. Military weapons—United States—Juvenile literature. I. Griffin, Margaret, MS. II. Fox, Barbara
J. III. Title.
UF23.S53 2013
623.4—dc23   2012004306

Summary: Describes the weapons and artillery used by the U.S. military.

Editorial Credits

Brenda Haugen, editor; Kyle Grenz, designer; Laura Manthe, production specialist

Photo Credits

Newscom: Itar-Tass Photos/Shirokov Andrey, 8-9, ZUMA Press, 17; U.S. Air Force photo by
Senior Airman Melissa V. Brownstein, 5, Staff Sgt. Eric Harris, 29, Staff Sgt. Russ Pollanen,
24-25, 25 (Both), Tech Sgt. Jeffery Allen, 26-27, Tech Sgt. Michael Ammons, 23 (Bottom); U.S.
Army photo, 10-11, 13 (Bottom), by PEOSoldier, cover (Top), Spc. Evan D. Marcy, 15, Spc.
Michael J. Macleod, 6-7, Ted Gaskins, 13 (Top); U.S. Marine Corps photo by Lance Cpl. Jacob W.
Chase, cover (Bottom), Cpl. Christopher R. Rye, 18-19, Cpl. Jeremy Ross, 20
Cpl. Patrick P. Evenson, 14, Cpl. Tyler W. Hill, 21, Gunnery Sgt. Bryce Piper, 28; U.S. Navy Photo
by MC3 Randall Damm, 27 (Bottom), PH3 Quinton Jackson, 23 (Top)

Artistic Effects

deviantart.com/Salwiak, backgrounds

Printed in the United States of America in
Stevens Point, Wisconsin.
032012   006678WZF12

TABLE OF CONTENTS

THE TOOLS OF WAR

The U.S. military has amazing weapons. Some old weapons are improved. Others are brand new. Come take a look!

CHAPTER 1

SMALL BUT MIGHTY

FACT The M320 is a stand-alone weapon
when it is not attached to a rifle.

The M320 Grenade Launcher attaches to an M16 or M4 Carbine rifle. The M320 launches **grenades** at targets such as buildings.

rifle

M320

grenade—a small bomb that can be thrown or launched

CornerShots are guns used in battles where there are many places to hide. The front part of the gun turns on a **hinge**. The gun has a video camera that shows a soldier what is around a corner.

video camera

hinge

hinge—a joint that allows something to turn or swing

XM25 rifles make it hard for enemies to hide. Grenades fired from these rifles travel over walls. The grenades explode when they reach a certain distance.

CHAPTER 2

ARTILLERY'S BIG GUNS

Soldiers drive **tracked** artillery such as the Multiple Launch Rocket System (MLRS) to firing **sites**. The MLRS fires 12 rockets, one after another.

tracked—having links that form an endless loop, like a conveyer belt or "rolling road"

site—the place where something is or happens

track

13

M777
Howitzer

A truck or helicopter moves the M777 Howitzer to a firing site. The Howitzer shoots large **shells** that hit targets up to 25 miles (40 kilometers) away.

FACT A five-member crew can have the Howitzer ready to fire in three minutes.

shell—a large bullet fired from a cannon

CHAPTER 3

ARMOR BUSTERS

The Javelin is a shoulder-fired cannon. It sends a **missile** high above an enemy tank. When the missile falls, it blasts the top of the tank where the **armor** is weakest.

missile—an explosive weapon that can travel long distances

armor—a protective metal covering

FACT The Javelin can also be fired at buildings and helicopters.

Javelin

missile

TOW missiles are launched from tubes on vehicles and helicopters. Enemy armored vehicles are the targets.

A soldier guides the missile by keeping the target in the **crosshairs** of a **sight.**

TOW missile

crosshairs—two lines inside a gun's sight that show where a gun is aimed

sight—a device that helps a person aim a gun

A tank shoots APFSDS shells. These shells punch holes in a tank's armor.

FACT APFSDS stands for "armor-piercing, fin-stabilized, discarding sabot." The U.S. military calls these shells "silver bullets."

CHAPTER 4

BRAINY WEAPONS

The Joint Direct Attack Munition kit makes a dumb bomb smart. A dumb bomb can't control where it lands. The kit gives a dumb bomb a **GPS**, fins, and a tail. These additions make a smart bomb that can be guided directly to a target.

WARNI

GPS—an electronic tool used to find the location of an object; GPS stands for global positioning system

Soldiers prepare to move a smart bomb.

A CAPTOR mine sits on the ocean floor. It uses **sonar** to sense an enemy submarine. It then releases a Mark 46 torpedo that bursts through the enemy submarine.

CAPTOR mine

NO LOAD

sonar—a device that uses sound waves to find underwater objects

WARNI

CAPTOR mines are delivered by submarine, ship, and aircraft.

CAPTOR mine

X28

U.S. fighter planes shoot
Sidewinder missiles at enemy planes.
These missiles sense heat from the
engine exhaust of enemy planes.

Sidewinder missile

A soldier does a safety check on a Sidewinder.

U.S. military weapons in the future will be even safer and smarter. These weapons will quickly strike targets without harming nearby areas.

Who knows what new high-tech weapon will be coming next?

GLOSSARY

armor (AR-muhr)—a protective metal covering

crosshairs (KRAWSS-hayrz)—two lines inside a gun's sight that show where a gun is aimed

GPS (JEE PEE ESS)—an electronic tool used to find the location of an object; GPS stands for global positioning system

grenade (gruh-NAYD)—a small bomb that can be thrown or launched

hinge (HINJ)—a joint that allows something to turn or swing

missile (MISS-uhl)—an explosive weapon that can travel long distances

shell (SHEL)—a large bullet fired from a cannon

sight (SITE)—a device that helps a person aim a gun

site (SITE)—the place where something is or happens

sonar (SOH-nar)—a device that uses sound waves to find underwater objects

tracked (TRAKT)—having links that form an endless loop, like a conveyer belt or "rolling road"

READ MORE

Alpert, Barbara. *U.S. Military Warships.* U.S. Military Technology. North Mankato, Minn.: Capstone Press, 2013.

Doeden, Matt. *Weapons of the Modern Day.* Weapons of War. Mankato, Minn.: Capstone Press, 2009.

Dougherty, Martin J. *Weapons and Technology.* Modern Warfare. Pleasantville, N.Y.: GS Learning Library, 2010.

INTERNET SITES

FactHound offers a safe, fun way to find Internet sites related to this book. All of the sites on FactHound have been researched by our staff.

Here's all you do:

Visit *www.facthound.com*

Type in this code: 9781429686143

Super-cool stuff!

Check out projects, games and lots more at
www.capstonekids.com

INDEX